# The Little Book Of Help

It's like therapy in a poem –
without the waiting list!

Samantha Lee

Copyright © Samantha Lee 2021
This book is sold subject to the condition that it shall not, by way of trade or otherwise, be lent, resold, hired out, or otherwise circulated without the publisher's prior consent in any form of binding or cover other than that in which it is published and without a similar condition including this condition being imposed on the subsequent publisher.
The moral right of Samantha Lee has been asserted.
ISBN-13: 9798783009259

*For Kiera
Always*

# CONTENTS

ACKNOWLEDGMENTS................................................................. i
INTRODUCTION ........................................................................ 1
PROLOGUE ................................................................................ 5
   *Here I Am* ............................................................................... 6

**Part I: GETTING READY FOR CHANGE**............................................. 7
   *Changes* .................................................................................. 8
   *F.I.N.E.* ..................................................................................... 9
   *Happy New Year*.................................................................... 10
   *The Mask*............................................................................... 12
   *The Crossroads*..................................................................... 13

**Part II: THE BEGINNING** ............................................................. 14
   *The Counsellor*...................................................................... 15
   *Time* ...................................................................................... 16

**Part III: THE MIDDLE BIT** ........................................................... 17
   **Bereavement & Loss**............................................................ 18
   *Loss* ........................................................................................ 19
   *Say My Name* ........................................................................ 21
   *Now you're not Here* ............................................................ 23
   *Should* ................................................................................... 25
   **Love and Relationships** ....................................................... 27
   *You think you know Me*........................................................ 28
   *Pretend*.................................................................................. 30
   *Heart* ..................................................................................... 31
   *Love's Song*........................................................................... 32

It's Time ................................................................ 34
**Low Self-Esteem** ................................................ 35
The Voice inside my Head ................................... 36
Amazing Self ........................................................ 38
If I was… ............................................................... 39
The Trophy ........................................................... 40
Anxiety & Panic Attacks ....................................... 41
**Anxiety** ................................................................ 42
My Frenemy .......................................................... 44
Panic at the Disco ................................................ 47
**Addiction** ............................................................. 50
The Mistress ......................................................... 51
Addiction is the Answer ....................................... 53
**Domestic Abuse** ................................................. 55
Love of My Life ..................................................... 56
**The Wounds of the Past: The Inner Child** ....... 59
The Child .............................................................. 60
Part of Me ............................................................. 61
The Secret ............................................................ 62
Boy to Man ........................................................... 63
Pass the Parcel .................................................... 65
**The Pandemic And World Events** ..................... 66
Apocalypse Now ................................................... 67
The Circus ............................................................ 68
Fear ....................................................................... 70
Beauty is in the Eye of the Beholder .................. 71

**Part IV: THE LIGHT AT THE END OF THE TUNNEL** ....... 73
Stop, Look, Listen ................................................ 74
The King of Words ............................................... 75
The Commuter ..................................................... 77
Just Talk ............................................................... 79

**Part V: THE OTHER SIDE** .................................................... 81
- *Cry* ........................................................................ 82
- *Where there is Life* ................................................. 84
- *Time for Change* .................................................... 85
- *Sit Tight* ................................................................. 86
- *That's Life* .............................................................. 87

**EPILOGUE** ............................................................... 89
- *I'm a Therapist But…* ............................................. 90
- *If I Knew* ................................................................ 91
- **Therapy – The Real Thing** ................................... 92

**ABOUT THE AUTHOR** ............................................. 94

# Acknowledgments

For my Therapist, Jeanette, who taught me how to hear my voice and find the words – thank you for introducing me to "Little Sam" – I promise to look after her.

For my Parents who have always done their very best with what they've had, and taught me kindness, resilience and so much more. Eternal love to you both.

For my Sister, whose never-ending love and support has always got me through all of the crappy bits and who makes me laugh whenever I see her – you are priceless to me.

For my Partner Rob, who is the positive to my negative and the one I finally want to get grey and wrinkly with.

And finally, for all the people who have hurt me in the past – I now see your wounds, I don't condone your various behaviours but I do understand them. Thank you for the lessons I learnt in what NOT to settle for. I'm worth so much more than that.

# Introduction

At the grand old age of 42, I found myself redundant after 20 years of working in London.

On top of that, I was fresh out of yet another failed relationship, and a single mum living on benefits. It's safe to say that Life Was Not Good!

To cut a very long story short, a chance conversation at this point in my life eventually led me to train as a Counsellor /Therapist, but before that?

Well, sometimes, I just felt like the loneliest person on the planet, even though I had a beautiful child, a loving family, and a wonderful group of friends.

I would compare myself to everyone else and always find myself lacking. I would look at my friends in their lovely homes with their seemingly lovely partners and feel bad for feeling jealous.

Part of me was happy but I'd hear this voice always saying, "Why can't I just find someone to take the pressure off and "make me happy?"

I feel sad when I look back at me then. At the time, I truly believed that I would only ever be happy and feel like everyone else, once I was with someone, so I kept choosing unhealthy relationships, putting my happiness in someone else's incapable hands.

I didn't realise that it was down to ME to make me happy.... *until I had therapy.*

I'd look back on my life and there always seemed to be large phases where I felt that Life Was Not Good!

Ok, some of it WAS good – I fell in love, I got engaged, I bought my first home, I had a career I loved. I'm sure there were a lot of people who looked at ME in the same way that I looked at them and maybe thought that I was the one who had the best life.

But from my perspective, the bad bits in my life always outstayed their welcome.

I'd started having anxiety and panic attacks at the age of 21. They slowly took over my life for the next few years.

I'd never heard of anxiety or panic attacks back then (this was in the early '90's when mental health wasn't really a thing). I just never considered asking for help to deal with them because quite frankly, I felt embarrassed. I didn't understand what the hell was going on and I genuinely feared that I was going mad.

There eventually came a day when I finally had one panic attack too many.

I got home from yet another failed attempt of trying to get on the train to work, sat in my lounge and had such a complete and utter petrifying emotional meltdown that I honestly felt like I was going to die.

A visit to a wonderful GP that day enabled me to slowly get back on track with the aid of an understanding ear and a bottle of anti-depressants, and although I never had another panic attack, anxiety stayed my loyal friend for the next 20 years.

The anti-depressants were only a practical "plaster". They levelled me out enough to feel like I could cope again. To this day, I find it amazing that I didn't ask anyone for help much earlier. I just felt like you had to "keep calm and carry on" and so that is what I tried to do, until I couldn't do it anymore.

But the thing is, for years, I never understood the root cause of WHY I had succumbed to anxiety and panic attacks.... *until I had therapy.*

I went on to experience a sudden bereavement at the age of 25 which rocked the foundations of my world to the core. I believe I got through it, eventually, but I didn't fully understand grief and the myriad of ways it can affect us....*until I had therapy.*

Moving on to relationships, and I developed a real skill for choosing all the wrong partners. It's a common problem when the world is full of emotionally wounded children walking around in adult bodies.

I never knew why, as a seemingly intelligent adult, I dismissed the genuinely nice guys, drawn instead to chaotic, drama filled relationships like a moth to the flame....*until I had therapy.*

It got to the point where there were so many questions I would ask myself – I sounded like the proverbial broken record.

- Why does this keep going wrong?
- Why can't I get this right?
- What's wrong with me?
- What's wrong with THEM?
- Why does this hurt so much?
- Why do I feel like THIS?
- Why do they feel like THAT?
- Why do I behave THIS way?
- Why do they behave THAT way?
- Why did that happen?"
- Why DIDN'T that happen?
- Why is there no-one here to do the washing up??

I never found the answers....*until I had therapy.*

So now many years later, as a therapist who has also been The Client, I am able to help other people find the answers to their very own unique and personal questions.

One of the ways that I make sense of the things both myself

and my clients have experienced is to write simple poems.

My poems condense the experiences we live through.

I've found that when we are emotionally overwhelmed, poetry can help. It can tackle life's difficult subjects and the related uncomfortable thoughts and feelings in a way that is easy to digest.

So, I've put all my poems together in "The Little Book of Help" to share some of my journey as both the Client and as the Therapist.

I want to show what I have learnt along the way about our struggles with Love, Loss, Relationships, Difficult Childhoods and more.

About the journey that more and more of us are now willing to travel with a therapist whilst we work out the answers to our own unique questions in life.

"The Little Book of Help" starts off gently. It might get painful in the middle but if you work your way through the "feely bit" maybe you'll come out the Other Side with new insight and a little inkling about what has happened to you in your life and why it may still be affecting you now.

I want the book to leave you feeling hope, comfort and positivity – things we all need to help us move forward in life.

I hope you enjoy "The Little Book of Help" - It's like therapy in a poem, but without the waiting list.

*Take care*

*Samantha Lee x*

# Prologue

## *Here I Am*

Here I am, a therapist sat opposite your chair
I wonder how you'd feel about the fact that I've sat there?
I too have been the client who has worked through grief and pain
In fact, I still sit in your chair when old wounds hurt again

Here I am, your therapist, I soothe and calm your fears
But sometimes I feel guilty when I still cry my own tears
When sometimes I still need someone to help me understand
That I don't have all the answers, sometimes need a helping hand

Here I am, a therapist who sometimes feels alone
My job, it sometimes stops me from just picking up the phone
From telling friends and family that I don't feel okay
I get too busy caring, and this job gets in the way

I worry if I tell them then I've failed in what I do
They'll think I cannot help myself so how can I help you
Yet whilst I have great knowledge, many skills to help me through
I'm human first so there are times I still don't have a clue

Therapists we may be, but I feel it's time to say
That firstly we ARE humans, we're NOT perfect, that's ok
We do not need perfection to be good at what we do
Accept your imperfections, after all they're what made YOU

So here I am, a therapist, I cry and struggle too
And when I fail, I learn and that is how I now help you
I don't regret my past; it's taught me everything I know
I may not be so perfect but can still help you to grow.

# Part I

# Getting Ready for Change

## *Changes*

I want to make some changes
I've been struggling for a while
Inside I feel unhappy
Yet to you I laugh and smile

I eat too much
It helps, to swallow chocolate with my tears
I drink too much
It helps, to numb the pain and drown my fears

I scrutinise the mirror
And I don't like what I see
So, I want to make some changes
And they need to start with me.

## F.I.N.E.

When people ask me how I am, I always smile and say
"I'm fine thanks, how are you?" and hope that sends them on their way
"I'm fine" is like a full stop, no more chat please, move along
The person asking doesn't really want to hear what's wrong

If I reply "I'm fine" it's 'cos I don't know how to say
"Well as you've asked, I'm having the most awful shitty day"
I don't know how to say "I'm sad and don't even know why,
But as you've asked, well some days all I do is sit and cry"

I worry that the person will then worry over me
And won't know what to say and won't know how they can help me
I find "I'm fine" is also good in helping fool myself
That I'm okay, there's nothing wrong, I have good mental health

They say that FINE it stands for

F eelings
I nside
N ot
E xpressed

I guess that's true, I don't tell anybody when I'm stressed
I don't talk through the things that in the past have made me sad
They then build up inside me, which is why I feel so bad

So, if you have a tendency for all of the above
Look for ways to find some words to share with those you love
They may well get upset, worried, feel unsure what to do
But reaching out, or reaching in, means they can help you through.

## Happy New Year

This coming year I vow to make big changes in my life
I can't keep eating too much food to deal with all my strife
If I can lose a stone or two then happiness will come
I'll feel a million dollars If I don't have a big bum!

I think I'll try Dry January to try and curb my drinking
I can't keep downing shots and wine to cancel out my thinking
I'm sure that if I go a month without a single glass
I'll prove I'm not a drunk who feels the need to numb the past

This coming year I plan on getting fit - I'll join the gym
I know I'll feel much better if I'm toned and fit and slim
If I can change my body then I know that I'll feel happy
That's sure to be the reason why I feel so bloody crappy

I'll make a better effort to get on with Mum or Dad
Meet up with friends more often - that will stop me feeling bad
I'll try to stop the arguments, be nice as pie for now
Ignore their crap behaviour so we don't get in a row

But have you ever thought about just why you eat too much?
Have you ever wondered why you use drink as a crutch?
Do you think "why is it that I don't look after me?"
"Why is it that I don't get on with friends and family?"

A diet will not solve the reason why you eat too much
Dry January won't stop you if you're drinking wine for lunch
100 workouts won't change how you think about yourself
Avoiding rows to keep the peace affects your mental health

So, make your New Years' promise, one that's different from the last
Try "Therapy" to look at what has happened in the past
You might just find the answers that make sense of how you feel
To make this year the one where you allow yourself to heal.

## *The Mask*

Us Brits have found a way that we've developed over time
To help us get through every day to make sure that we're fine
We've got so good at doing what we do to hide the fact
That inside we feel unhappy, what you see is just an act

We wear a mask you see, it's one we put on every day
The mask, it wears a smile that tells you all that "I'm ok"
The mask it laughs and smiles at you, it's happy and content
But the person underneath is feeling absolutely spent

Before they wore the mask you'd ask them "tell me how you feel"
But the pain of truth brought feelings that they didn't want made real
So the beauty of the mask means they can hide at peace behind
The bravest face, the brightest smile, to hide their troubled mind

Their mask is like a blanket that they love to hide beneath
To keep them warm, to keep them safe from feeling any grief
But masks, they slip and then the face that's real is there to see
So it's time to drop the mask and face the pain to set it free

No need to be the strong one, it's okay to have a cry
No need to keep pretending you're okay, no need to lie
Be honest how you're feeling, shed a tear and face your pain
Once it's dealt with, you can drop that mask and be yourself again.

## *The Crossroads*

I'm standing at the crossroads of a path that splits in two
One path leads to a place called "Safe", the other path's called "New"
Today I want to try and walk the new path, see what's there
But as I face the new path, there's a voice I hear that's scared

Do not go there, it tells me, this is Risky, Scary, Bad!
You don't know where it goes to, what it leads to - are you mad?
Why are you going somewhere that you don't know what's in store?
Let's take the path to "Safe" again, we've been down there before

I'm bored with "Safe!" I shout aloud, it keeps me in a trap
It stops me from progressing and it leaves me feeling crap
"Safe" isn't where I want to go, I want to walk down "New"
But each time that I start to walk, I bump right into you!

This inner voice protects me from the things that may bring fear
It's scared of change, of losing all the things I hold so dear
The voice is scared to fail, of being different from the rest
It stops me reaching for the sky, to do what I think's best

Sometimes a risk is needed, reassure that voice from old
That the Adult you has got the skills to reach your pot of gold
Your Inner Child will worry, old vulnerabilities will loom
But step outside your comfort zone and watch a new life bloom

So here I stand at Crossroads while I listen to that voice
I know now that it's time to change, I have to make a choice
To walk down "Safe" is comforting but "New" is what I see
"Be brave, you know you've got this" and I smile and follow Me.

# Part II

# The Beginning

## *The Counsellor*

You don't know me, I don't know you, we've never met before
Two total strangers weeks ago, before you found my door
What made you choose my photo then? What made you think
"That's her"
The one I'll tell my story to - she'll make me feel secure

What secrets you bestow on me, what trust you put in me
To find a space to talk in that feels safe to set pain free
To trust that I can help you in a way that gives release
A way that over time will give you hope and give you peace

The keeper of your secrets, the witness to your story
The one who sees and feels your pain in all its' awful glory
An honour like no other, to be given trust like this
To keep you in a safe place as you face your own abyss

The one who over time can see you change and see you grow
The one who keeps on listening 'til you're confident to go
And live your life with new eyes, with a vision that is clear
A new you – something priceless that us Counsellors hold dear

They call us wounded healers; did you know that to be true?
We've all "been there" in some way and have found our own way through
We've all had our own journey that has taught us what we know
So, thank you for your trust in us - we hope we help you grow.

## *Time*

Is time a gift for you, a space for thought, to stop, reflect
Or just a dirty window to view sorrow and regret?
Do you use Time to work out things that mean the most to you
Or does Time underline the things that you still struggle through?

Is Time the biggest healer, space to mourn and shed a tear
Or is it your worst enemy, a space where you feel fear?
Does Time give you connection to the people you hold dear
Or does it represent a wall to stop them coming near?

Does Time offer a place for you to slow down, sleep and rest
Or fill the minutes up so you don't have to feel distress?
Is Time a sunny blue sky, days spent loving life's mad ride
Or is it a dark blanket under which you stay and hide?

Time, it can be such a gift, it really does depend
On whether life has taught you it's an enemy or friend
Each one of us gets given the same hours every day
It's up to us to spend them in the most fulfilling way

Don't fill your Time with too much "stuff" to block pain from your mind
Or Time becomes your enemy - it won't be very kind
Whilst full minds might not feel the pain you've buried underneath
Whenever you have Time alone, you'll feel the grief beneath

If Time is used to give you space each day to stop and breathe
You'll find a space to process each emotion, watch it leave
Time spent alone will then become a Best Friend and a pleasure
Each hour spent alone, a gift for you to love and treasure.

# Part III

# The Middle Bit

# Why do I feel like this?

Tell me, what has HAPPENED to you?

*Bereavement & Loss*

## *Loss*

My world does not make sense today
There's something not quite right
A feeling that there's something wrong
My world has lost its' light

I've woken up, I don't feel me
I don't feel you, just space
You filled it only yesterday
Now look, an empty place

The $1^{st}$ of firsts now start today
$1^{st}$ day of losing you
$1^{st}$ day of being me alone
How will it be? No clue

Loss, a harmless little word
Until I feel it's' power
Consuming every thought I have
Destroying every hour

No care for how it steals my joy
It will not be ignored
I try to run away from it
But no, it has me floored

Distract myself, keep busy
Fool myself that I'm okay
But Loss, it follows patiently
To bite another day

I know that I must hold its' hand
And let me guide it through
The anger, churning bleakness

Yearning desperate need of you

If I can sit inside my Loss
Respect it, feel it's' force
In time, we'll go our separate ways
Let life take its' new course

This life will feel so different now
Without you there to see
And loss will visit now and then
To sit alongside me

Reminding me that I've survived
To use what I've been through
To love and comfort others
When their life is torn in two.

## *Say My Name*

There was a time in years gone by
Your name was like a kiss
So often was it on my lips
But now something's amiss

I try to speak, to talk of you
Because my love's still there
I want to talk of good times
And the life we used to share

But loved ones, friends, and family
They rarely speak your name
They worry that they'll make me cry
They're scared to cause me pain

So, silence is our dress code
And we blindly follow suit
Your name is never mentioned
Nothing, silence, pressed to mute

My pain repressed gets bigger
When denied a voice, it breeds
It grows like grass in Summer
Leaves my heart covered in weeds

My loss is nothing dirty
Something bad to hide away
The more that I can speak of you
The more grief goes away

So let me say your name out loud
Allow another tear
So, I can grieve and find a way
To live without you here

## *Now you're not Here*

It's that time of year when your absence is felt
More keenly than at any other time
I remember when I was so much a part of your life
And you made up so much of mine

A time where your presence was a given
You were always there, that's just how it was
And how it was meant to be
You and me

I didn't allow myself to think of a life without you,
Well, maybe sometimes, but it always made me ache
So, I'd wave the thoughts away, file them under "pending"
An impossible thought to think of "us" ever ending

Save it for another day,
When you really weren't here,
Another time, another place, when I could no longer see your
dear face
Or hold you close to me

Memories of you
Sometimes it feels like they are the only thing
That make my heart remember what it's there for
It can feel like it just beats out of habit

But when I allow myself to think of you
I feel my heart expand
I think it feels the warmth of your love and remembers its
purpose
That's why you not being here leaves such a space
My love for you took up a lot of room

That's what I hold on to at times like this
The memory of your love and how it felt to be loved by you
Now you're not here, your love is no longer tangible
But it's a feeling of feelings

Happiness, laughter, warmth, belonging
Sometimes grief, pain, longing
But overall, a beautiful feeling that reminds me
That I loved you and I was loved by you
Then for a while, the pain gets smothered by the warmth of that love

No matter how long I live without you
The love we had, we will always have
It lives inside me every day, it will never go away
I promise.

## *Should*

You brought me into your world
I did not ask to be there
You should have been my dad
But no, your love was never shared

You brought me into your world
There was no choice there for me
You should have been my mum
You failed, that name you couldn't be

"My Dad" - a label filled with love
The one who has your back
But all I got from you
Was hurt and pain, a heart that cracked

"My Mum" - the one whose kisses, hugs
Are meant to soothe your pain
Were gifts you never gave me
Just rejection, hate and shame

I never cease to wonder
Why on earth you had a child
Your lives were so chaotic
Past wounds still ran deep and wild

So many take for granted
What a mum and dad should be
But I have only ever known
A fractured family

I mourn the loss of love denied
One every child should feel
I mourn for you, my mum and dad
Part of me loves you still.

*Love and Relationships*

## *You think you know Me*

You think you know me, but you don't
This front is made for you
I've built it over many years
So, no one can see through

I've built this wall with many bricks
To make it big and strong
Then painted it with laughs and smiles
So, you can't see what's wrong

You think you know me, but you don't
I've learnt to hide my fears
With work and keeping busy
So, there's no time for my tears

If I allowed the wall to break
And you could see straight through
I wonder if you'd love the soul
Now stood in front of you

The one you thought was happy
Full of confidence and strength
Who's spent their whole life hiding
Their true self at any length

For having built my wall of steel
To hide what I can see
The thing I yearn for most in life
Is someone to love me

With all my imperfections
All the things I hide from you
I want to know you see my faults
But still say "I love you".

## *Pretend*

Today I stand in adulthood, a grown man, "big and strong"
So why is it that I now feel my whole life's going wrong?
I've spent so long believing that men aren't supposed to cry
We all pretend, keep calm, but now I'm sat here thinking "Why?"

Why can't I show my pain to you whenever I feel sad?
Why can't I show my anger if you've hurt me and I'm mad?
Why can't I show my sadness when love leaves and I'm left reeling?
Why can't I just be honest, tell you how I'm truly feeling?

Just when was it decided that a man must not show fear?
And why was it concluded that it's weak to shed a tear?
I have a heart, I'm human, I still feel the same as you
Why can women cry, but as a man……? No that won't do.

My whole life I have had to take each blow, hide it away
Be the rock for others but to hide my own dismay
Pretend it never hurts, and if it does, put on a show
To make it seem that I'm okay, so no-one ever knows

So, look at me pretend, my heart is sagging with the weight
Of unexpressed emotions I was taught not to relate
I've kept them hidden all this time, I have to make a choice
End my life to end this pain…..? or somehow find my voice?

Give myself permission to revise this old belief
Show my vulnerabilities and feel the pure relief
Of showing that I have a heart, it's not one made of stone
Teach men to stop pretending - we don't have to cope alone.

## *Heart*

Bless my gentle, loving heart
It's lost its' shape today
The love that made it feel so full
Got up and walked away

That tender touch that made it skip
The love that made it swell
Has turned into a viscous punch
Left pain I cannot quell

My gentle heart has fallen
Laying heavy on its' side
Your parting kick has ripped it
Left a gaping wound inside

The trust that kept it warm has gone
I barely feel it there
The beat has lost its' strength
It flounders knowing you don't care

Dear Heart, you're stronger than you think
You may feel like this now
But life has taught me hearts repair
They learn to heal somehow

For now, though gentle, loving heart
It's time for you to grieve
Let sadness hold your loving curves
'til once more you can breathe.

## Love's Song

I miss you
I hate you
I love you
Berate you

You pushed me away
Yet I want you to stay
I need one more day
Of us

I miss you; I hate you
Adore you
Abhor you
Don't need you, but want you
Wish you were here, My Dear

You hurt me, Desert me
Then come back and leave
I lay in this emptiness
Wounded

I love me, I miss me
I left for a while, for your smile
I love me, I miss me, I'm coming back
With a heart that's now cracked

I loved you, I missed you
But I've kissed you goodbye
I broke for a while
For your smile

I look forward - I move on
I look back - I crack
I stand still
And I feel

Hurts for a while
When I think of your smile
But this is love's' song
We move on.

## *It's Time*

You're telling me it's over and I have to say goodbye
Another one I've loved and lost no matter how I've tried
I thought I'd got it right this time, I thought the love was there
But for you the light had gone out and your heart was feeling bare

We spend our years pursuing love, we need to feel it's' strength
At first when we are looking we will go to any length
To find The One to be with, sometimes scared to tell them "No"
We compromise our needs to make sure that they'll never go

We doubt our own survival when love dies and goes away
We wonder if our broken heart will beat another day
Yet through the raw pain, bleakness, sadness on our knees we crawl
Until the day we realise that we're okay after all

Each loss that you survive, it hurts and takes a piece of you
But learn the lessons left by all the pain that you've been through
Look back at any unmet needs you'd learnt to live without
So, when you meet a new love they are things to talk about

To make sure that this new love is an upgrade on the last
With all the things you loved but without all the damaged parts
It's time to love yourself, to give your heart the things it needs
For self-love is the food on which a healthy heart will feed.

# Low Self-Esteem

## *The Voice inside my Head*

When I think back through the years gone by, of how I've treated you
It makes me sad to think of things I've said that just weren't true
Of times when you've been vulnerable and needed my advice
I've not been very kind and now your self- worth's paid the price

So many times, you've asked me how you've looked, I've felt disgust
And left you feeling crap and like there's no one you could trust
You've asked me if you're getting fat - I've laughed and got more wine
Have another glass I've said, you'll soon be feeling fine

There's been times when you've been honest, told me that you're feeling sad
I've told you "Just get on with it, or friends will think you're mad!"
I've let you struggle on until you've found it hard to cope
And still I wasn't kind to you, I didn't give you hope

And yet you are the person that I need to love the most
The one life I should celebrate, the one that I should toast
The one who's always been there by my side my whole life through
So why is it I'm so unkind when talking down to you?

Because that "you" is me you see, the voice that's in my head
The one that pulls me down each day, whose voice fills me with dread
The one who criticises me for things I'll never be
The voice is mine and it's so cruel because I don't love me

Beliefs we think about ourselves aren't always true today
They're often replayed messages our young selves used to say
The thoughts believed in childhood shape the adult that we are
But old beliefs must be revised or else they leave a scar

So, change that inner voice to one who loves the Adult you
Love wrinkles, imperfections, past mistakes, they're lessons too
The voice we listen to the most is ours, make sure it's kind
For to love yourself each day ensures you'll keep a healthy mind.

## *Amazing Self*

When I compare myself to other people that I see
I always make assumptions that they're way better than me
I look at things I've worked on, things I'm proud that I've achieved
But then I look at others work, begin to feel aggrieved

I start to doubt my efforts, slowly pick them all apart
Chastise myself for thinking I was good enough to start
A project that excited me, a great business idea
I'm sure that I can do it but then start to feel "The Fear"

"The Fear" that I will fail, "The Fear" that I'm not Good Enough
"The Fear" you'll find my weaknesses, and see I'm not so tough
You'll say I don't belong; I just don't fit in with your kind
And this is just the start of all the thoughts stuck in my mind

I feel like an imposter, one who doesn't really see
The merit in my work, or what you really think of me
Too quick am I to tear down any compliment I hear
Too quick to give up trying – your rejection's what I fear

I fail myself by not believing just what I can do
I fail myself when I compare myself right next to you
Why compare how your life is when stood up next to mine?
Comparison, the thief of joy – it's such a waste of time!

A waste of time as maybe this is something you don't see
I compare myself to you, you do the same with me
And everybody in the world compares with someone else
Let's stop! Just celebrate what makes your own Amazing Self.

## *If I was...*

If I was your best friend, would you say I looked a state
Tell me I'm a mess and that my clothes are second rate?
Run me down and tell me that my hair's a dreadful mess
Tell me what a sight I look whenever I get dressed?

If I was your best friend, would you stop me doing well
Make me keep a job I hate that makes me feel like hell?
Keep me with a Partner who has no respect for me
Who tells me what to wear and tells me who I cannot see?

If I was your best friend would you tell me that I'm fat
Hate me 'cos my stomach isn't perfect, isn't flat?
Think that I am worthless based on looks or shape or size
Tell me I'm not sexy based upon my flabby thighs?

Well, here I stand, your Best Friend and I'm looking straight at you
You're right here in my mirror and it's time to start anew
You'd never treat your best friend in the way that you treat me
So, now's the time to change, it's time you started loving me.

## *The Trophy*

If I could get a trophy for the things I've failed to do
I'd need a trophy cabinet to show them all to you
I'm sure you'll recognise the things I fail at every day
As no doubt you have trophies of your own you could display

I fail when people ask me "How are You?" I say "I'm fine"
When all I want to do is blub and pour myself some wine
I'm as far away from fine that it is possible to get
But I keep it to myself because I don't want you to fret

I fail with the crying thing; it feels so hard to do
It makes me feel so sad and like my heart has split in two
I swallow down my sadness hiding how I really feel
'Cos to feel my own emotions makes them far too bloody real

I fail at reaching out when I need help and feel alone
What stops me reaching out to you, just picking up the phone?
I'm sorry I can't answer that, I fail at talking too
It's why I feel so sad at times, I can't reach out to you

And so finally I fail at pleasing everyone I see
I try to keep them happy but then where does that leave me?
Feeling unappreciated, lonely, undervalued, sad
So I fail at feeling good and end up feeling really bad

Now if you've won a trophy for the things I've mentioned here
Shall we make a pact to change the things we fail at, end it here?
Let's win trophies being honest, being open, that's a start
As to share what's on our mind ensures we keep a happy heart.

*Anxiety & Panic Attacks*

## *Anxiety*

Anxiety, my enemy, I hate you with a passion
You're so in vogue these days, I wear you like the latest fashion
You spoil so many people's lives, you make me feel such fear
Over absolutely nothing when there's no real danger near

You make me wake each morning with a fear I've come to dread
You make my heartbeat fast; I feel I can't get out of bed
You make me breathe too quickly, make me feel there's no more air
You make me feel so terrified, I feel I've been stripped bare

Stripped bare of logic, reason, my behaviour goes so weird
Avoiding people, places, things I never used to fear
You tamper with my mind and make me feel I'm going mad
I flit from feeling petrified to vulnerable then sad

So, what makes you so utterly horrendous to endure
What is it about you that makes me feel so insecure?
How is it that when you arrive, I feel my world might end
When I'm fearful, feeling lonely, like I haven't got a friend?

You take me back sometimes to how I felt when I was young
Where the skills to deal with problems in my life had not yet sprung
A helpless little child needing an adult to be there
Someone to keep me safe from harm, to show a bit of care

Anxiety can feed on vulnerability and grief
So, if you feel it, maybe there's some past loss underneath
Too often we avoid the pain we don't work our way through
Then wonder why years later we are enveloped by you

So, if Anxiety is making life feel bad for you
Reach out, get help to talk about what life has led you through
As adults we now have the skills to deal with change and pain
It's Time to Talk, take charge reclaim your old self once again.

## *My Frenemy*

Just when you think you've got your life sorted
That you're heading in the right direction and feeling happy and confident in who you are
Up pops that toxic friend from the past
You love them, but you know they're not good for you

You've tried all kinds of ways to accept them, but they leave you feeling drained
They're needy – they can stop you from going out seeing friends, going on holiday, eating out
They've stopped you from going to work and at their worst
Have made you feel like you were truly going mad

You've tried time and again to get rid of them
Each time they go away, you think you've cracked it
That they've finally realised you don't need them around
But they know you so well

When all is good and you're striving forward, they turn up like a bad penny
"Hi, remember me" they say
And once again, even though you love them, you despise their behaviour
They manage to creep into your life, taking control

Start pushing all the good stuff away from your reach
"Don't try that, it's too scary"
"Don't do that, it's not good enough"
"Don't say that, people will laugh"

And so, they break your confidence down and stop you in your tracks again
The only way they ever go away
Is when you confront them
You can't hide from them you see; you can't pretend they're not there

"I see you friend, and you scare the hell out of me!
You can try every trick in the book to stop me from growing
But despite how you can make me feel
I'm not listening to you anymore - you're not going to control me anymore!"

"Despite the fear you bring out in me
I'm still going to do what I want to do
I'm still going to go where I want to go
I'm still going to become the person I know I can be!"

They don't like that because fear is their only weapon
You might know my friend yourself – their name is Anxiety
The reason I can't help but love them is because they are part of me
They are my past doubts and fears

The things that scared me as a child
Because naturally I didn't have the skills to deal with scary situations back then
I had parents/carers to help keep me safe
But I'm not a child anymore

The fears I used to have are no longer relevant in my adult life
I have the skills to manage what comes my way
So, when I try something new and scary, my old friend Anxiety tries to 'rescue' me
Tries to persuade me to stick with what I know to stay safe
But what a very small life we would live if we all stayed 'safe'

So next time Anxiety comes calling, tell them that you're fine
Tell them you don't need their help anymore
And if their presence still leaves you feeling a little scared, just say a quick "Hi" to them
But then, take a leap of faith into the life you want to live.

## *Panic at the Disco*

A normal day was to become the way that you'd show me what you could do
Me fine one minute, happy and calm, the next petrified, utterly, utterly petrified
Of what? I hadn't a clue
It was just "you"

That way you would finger your fear up my neck
Tightening my scalp like a Dagenham Facelift
Squeezing my head with a vice like grip
Until my head felt light and I thought I just might…. pass out

'Cos my heart, it would start to rave wildly in my chest
Like panic at the disco – utter chaos playing to a chaotic beat under my breast
A tune I'd come to dread and fear because when you were near I could hear the rate of my heart

I would start to breathe in such an unnatural way
It has left a scar to this very day
The memory of you can still squeeze my lungs so tightly when stressed
But you no longer have the power to control me so lightly

That breathing. God, it was like I'd just run a 100-metre sprint
But from the safety of my own chair - I hadn't run anywhere
But I felt like I wanted to run like Forest Gump and never look back
I just never knew what the hell it was I wanted to run away from?

You? Me?

That answer didn't come for another 20 odd years
But that's another story that will only take the glory away
From your 15 minutes of fame.
I digress!

The cherry on top of the cake that is you
Was the obsession I built with needing the loo
I just HAD to be where I could see it!

Me and Armitage Shanks became lovers
I'd sneak in to see him to hide from "the others"
Who didn't feel like they were losing their mind
With Shanks in full view, I felt safe. Safe from what?
I had no idea, that bit was always unclear

I guess he sheltered me from the **perceived** fear

I'd sit there and wait for the panic to abate
I could then leave without shaking and go back to faking that I
was perfectly
Fine, Fine, FINE!

I lived through those years waiting for something JUST SO
TERRIBLE to happen

There I would be in the most innocent of places, full of kind faces
But in my head, I just knew
If I couldn't get off that train, out of that shop, off that plane
Then that would be it, I'd be lost to you

Soon, the only place I felt safe was my home - my Safe Zone.

But after a while, you even took that away from me
That final day, another attempt at trying to get on the train to
work
But you wouldn't allow me to - I tried and I cried but I couldn't

So, I made my way home, I'd never felt so alone, I cried and I sobbed, I felt robbed

Of the life I'd once had, of the woman I'd been, I felt like a child again, helpless
And you chose that same day to finish the job as I started to sob you got me
To a point so low I had nowhere to go
You'd won and I let you feast on the remains of me ... for a while

But when you've reached rock bottom, the only way is up
The fighter in me wasn't done yet
With help, a different tune started to play in my chest
A beat of hope that I could come out of this stronger

No longer Panic at the Disco, more an anthemic "I will Survive" number
Whilst I tentatively danced around my handbag

I began to realise that no matter if it FELT like I was dying, I never did
It might have FELT like I'd never stop crying, but I did
It might have FELT like something JUST SO TERRIBLE would happen
But, *it never did*

I came to realise you were a liar
You'd made me think you were so scary
But you were all mouth and no trousers in the end
No more than a bully

Seeming so strong on the outside but with no inner strength
Not like me
You may have attacked me hundreds, maybe thousands of times
But here's the thing Panic Attack

I......SURVIVED.......EVERY.........SINGLE........ONE.......OF......YOU.

*Addiction*

## *The Mistress*

When I first met you and saw how much you loved her
I thought "Great! I love her too!"
She was such a laugh
We would always have so much fun with her

When we were in her company, there was just something about her
She allowed both of us to drop our inhibitions
Be who we wanted to be, she was so seductive
Bringing out the best in us, we were hilarious!

But slowly the relationship altered, went off keel
You started spending more time with her than I did
She'd started to lose her shine for me
And that's when she made her move

You started seeing her in secret
I had my suspicions, but I couldn't find the proof
Day by day, week by week, month by month
I saw you falling hook, line, and sinker

I pleaded with you to leave her
Choose me, I begged, I love you!
But my words were lost on you
Because you'd already lost yourself to her

You weren't her first, she's an experienced lover
She steals loved ones away all the time
You beg them to stay, you can't believe they are leaving you for her
But they will leave every single person they love rather than be without her

Who is she, this beautiful woman?
What does she have that I don't?
Well, let me tell you The Mistress ain't no Lady
Her real name is Alcohol Addiction……and she's a

        B rutal
        I solating
        T raumatising
        C haotic
        H ell

## *Addiction is the Answer*

Addiction is the answer, what's the question? I don't know!
I never thought to ask - it's just the first place that I go
Whenever I can think and feel I go and look for you
The substance of my choice? A bet? A purge? Yep, that'll do

Addiction is the answer, what's the question? Is there pain?
It's always there unless I use addiction once again
Addiction is my friend you see, a beautiful disguise
It offers a distraction from those old unanswered cries

Addiction is my keeper, it is always there for me
Unlike the help I needed when pain first came after me
An instant comfort blanket in the form of drink or drugs
Gambling, Anorexia, they take the place of hugs

Addiction helps me out when no-one else hears what I say
Addiction is reliable, it turns up every day
To soothe me when I'm hurting, wipes away my many tears
To numb my pain and blank my mind of memories and fears

Addiction is the answer, what's the question? Where's the love?
Where were you when I needed you when life got so damn tough?
To sort through things that I was just too young to comprehend
Why weren't you there to comfort, be my parent or my friend?

Addiction is the answer, but the question I now ask
Is "Do I want to love the soul who hides behind this mask"
The mask of my Addiction makes me hide the pain I feel
But hiding it denies it's there, I need to make it real

Take steps to find the courage to explore what's in my mind
Find someone who'll be there, to help me face it, to be kind
To show me it's okay to walk through pain without a crutch
A life free of addiction is a life that's worth so much.

*Domestic Abuse*

## *Love of My Life*

At a time in my life when things felt wrong, at a time when I didn't feel right
Where every day was a fight
To get out of bed and be the one in charge, responsibility weighed me down
I felt like a member of the "It's not Fair Club" and the "Life's so Hard Brigade"

As the newly single, Single Mum who felt jealous of everyone who had a man "looking after them"
Who didn't have to go home to find all the jobs still not done
Patiently waiting for my attention alone
'Cos no-one else was coming home to help me

You came along to "rescue" me, a knight in shining armor made up of promises and flattery
Who readily made me a princess and put me on a pedestal
Your words soothed my insecurities and vulnerable soul with declarations of a love like no other
Who swore that no-one would ever love me like you could
I was your best, I could forget the rest

The honeymoon period was bliss, I told myself, but My Self was lying
I'd had moments of doubt about some of your words - they'd stuck in my mind as unkind
But needy love stays blind, it doesn't want to see the cracks when they show
I knew that to "see" and acknowledge my thoughts would mean going back to being alone

Alone with my "old partner" - the Self-Esteem of a younger me
I'd have to live again with that familiar inner voice
Who carelessly whispers the same old shit like a broken record

"You're not good enough, you're different, you don't really belong" goes the song
"Be thankful you've got him; you might not get someone else"
The fact was I didn't have the courage to choose my Partners, I mostly waited to be chosen
"Put up with his ways and he'll take care of you"
"It's better than being alone" inner voice droned

That voice was wrong, but when you're worn down with old beliefs
She who shouts loudest, is the first to be heard - and she was
So, the choice was made, I stayed rather than be alone
Despite being fully grown, I listened to the child in me who wanted to be looked after
She wasn't brave enough to do "Adulting" - she needed a man to do that

I stayed another day, another month, another year
Until everything I held dear was a weapon used against me to stay
Don't leave me, you'd cry, I'm so sorry, I love you
Please stay, give me one last time, we'll be fine, remember, you're mine

But the more you tried to hold all the power, the more you tried to control
The more love failed to stick around - it left, long before I did
The day finally came, no more different than others but this time
I heard another voice from the past - At last
A voice drowned out by the scared younger me who didn't believe she was able

To be truly happy and safe without the love of a man to help keep her stable
But the voice on that day who showed me the way was my adult self

Shouting
**"Yes you can!"**

The voice who never believed that old song, the one who knew that old story was wrong
The one who has learnt to manage alone and knows she is perfectly able to provide a good home
And she does, and she has, all along
On her own

So, if you find yourself stuck in a life or a place that doesn't quite fit
Then listen to "me" - the "me" in your head who is still listening to an old song that is wrong
A song full of lines from your past that don't fit with the new lyrics you've re-written as you've grown
Listen to your new song, believe it, live it and sing it out loud and proud.

BE the Love of Your Life

*The Wounds of the Past*

*The Inner Child*

## *The Child*

I want to introduce you to a child that you once knew
I think you'll really love them, as they seem a lot like you
The tales they have remind me of the things that you tell me
The way they think, the way they act, I know that you'll agree

Tread carefully, they're vulnerable, be mindful what you say
They'll need to feel they're safe with you, build trust to feel okay
They've spent a lot of time alone; they often feel unheard
I've said you'll hear their story - will you listen to their words?

You may find that it's very hard to witness what they say
You'll see the world from their eyes, and feel sad they think that way
I know their words will cause you pain, but somehow give relief
As their pain will feel familiar, like a well-worn coat of grief

I want to introduce you to this child that you once knew
They've waited long enough for me to build this path for you
So, walk along and find a place where both of you can stand
To face your past together as you hold each-others' hand.

## *Part of Me*

We've lived together all these years; I've loved and hated you
Most days you're kind and loving, yet sometimes your tongue is cruel
Friends, they think they "know" you, but they don't see what I see
They think you're happy, confident, this other part of me

They look at what your life is like, they think you've got it all
Yet if I told them what I knew, they don't know you at all
I know the wounded parts that you've ignored for all these years
But you just refuse to listen when I try to voice my fears

I watch you keep on hiding me - I know I cause you shame
You think that I'll embarrass you - my memory causes pain
I trigger old beliefs that you no longer want to hear
You've tried to hide the real me as my presence causes fear

You cover bad behaviours that I use to deal with pain
But all it does is ensure that I'll use them all again
I bring up thoughts about you that are warped beliefs, untrue
For they made such perfect sense when living as the younger you

I am your wounded Inner Child, always alone and scared
I need for you to love me and to show me that you care
I need for you to hear my voice, correct my warped beliefs
Protect and love me always so that I can heal my grief.

## *The Secret*

I have a secret story; I have kept it quiet for years
I've been good and kept it locked away, along with all my tears
I've never told a soul but there is something about you
That helps me think I'll be ok to tell my secret to

I have a secret story, I'm ashamed to tell it now
It's always felt so wrong, as if I was to blame somehow
I don't know why it happened, but it felt so very bad
They told me it was all my fault and that's what makes me sad

I don't know how it happened and I'm not sure what they did
I didn't understand it, I was just a little kid
The worst thing was I knew them, and I thought they were a friend
But a friend would never do that, so their friendship was pretend

I have a secret story and the thing I need the most
Is to tell it somewhere safe so I can lay to rest this ghost
It's haunted me for years now, I just need to hear you say
The Three words "I believe you" then I know I'll be okay.

## *Boy to Man*

I'm looking in the mirror and reflected back at me
Is an Adult hearing voices of the Child I used to be
An Adult making choices based on echoes from the past
It's wrecking my relationships, they never seem to last

I'm drowning in this grown-up world; my actions leave me reeling
There are times I have no real clue as to what it is I'm feeling
An innocent remark can make me feel I want to cry
I'm a child who needs their Mum who's never there to wipe tears dry

I'm a child who fell and hurt himself, but no-one ever knew
The pain it caused back then and all the hurt that I went through
Beliefs I formed about myself back then never amended
My pain fell on deaf ears, left unresolved as childhood ended

So, into Adulthood the damaged child creeps in unseen
To play out old reactions on repeat just like a dream
This Inner child takes charge and tries to manage adult strife
But his skills are immature, they just don't work in Grown Up Life

He feels that he's not good enough compared to all his friends
He doesn't trust relationships; he fears they'll always end
A damaged child whose biggest fear is being left alone
To cope in this Big World without a place to call his home

I'm looking in the mirror and the grown man that I see
Is the key to heal this broken child, I need to set him free
To listen to his story and become the Mum or Dad
Who listens to his past pain, give the hug he never had

To reassure the child that he is loved now he's a man
To tell him that I love him every moment that I can
To let him grow inside of me, to never be alone
To love my Inner Child, give him my heart to call his home.

## *Pass the Parcel*

Remember when as children, Parents often drove you mad
The things they said and did could sometimes hurt and leave you sad
You swore you'd never be like them, you'd do things differently
But now you see the apple didn't fall far from the tree

Disappointment fills you as you slowly start to see
Bad history repeat itself in your own family
You've somehow turned out just the same, you've copied their mistakes
A trigger from your own child can be all the fuel it takes

To set off a re-action from an old fight with your Mum
As words ring in your ears of a past battle never won
A war of verbal weaponry, hearts ripped then bitter tears
And on it goes, repeat the loop, grief passed down through the years

We all play pass the parcel with old wounds we've never healed
They fester behind silent lips unless the truth's revealed
So, talk about your childhood, all the things that caused you pain
Or you'll just play pass the parcel and hurt gets passed on again.

*The Pandemic*

*And*

*World Events*

## *Apocalypse Now*

What the heck is going on, the world has gone quite mad
It feels like the Apocalypse, the news is really bad
A virus has us in its' grip, there's terror everywhere
Our vulnerable are dying, there is panic and despair

People panic buying, being kind, some have forgotten
An "I'm alright Jack" attitude makes some folk really rotten
Loo roll is as rare as rocking horse poo, so I'm told
To find a pack of Andrex is more valuable than gold!

From elderly and vulnerable we now must stay away
We can't pop round to see them, check they're safe and feel okay
No routine for our children now that school life's' had to end
No daily meets to have a chat, or hug a much-loved friend

We must now distance socially, the hardest part of all
For contact with our loved ones is what helps us when we fall
It really is a time that will now test the human mind
A task made so much easier if people can be kind

We're all in this together, let's now see what we can do
To reach out and protect the folk who need help to get through
I know it will be truly hard to get through every day
But together we are strong, let's send Corona on its' way!

## *The Circus*

I feel I've been propelled into a world that's lost its' purpose
I feel like I'm a monkey who's been made to join a circus
The audience are sat there with no clue what's going on
And they're really not enjoying it, the show's completely wrong

Last month it ran so perfectly, performers knew their place
They all knew what their role was, now that's really not the case
The jugglers have dropped their balls, their plates have all stopped spinning
The clowns have all stopped laughing now, not one of them is grinning

They've all been told "be careful" – there's a virus in the air
It's something we can't see but nonetheless we know it's there
We want to leave the big top 'cos we don't like this new show
But the Ring Master won't let us, it's not safe to let us go

So now we watch a new show, one we've never seen before
We watch the different acts unfold whilst safely tucked indoors
We start to see that some new acts are doing really well
But for many this new circus is a total living hell

Some are finding different ways to keep their act alive
They make the new show interesting - we sit and watch them thrive
But sadly, there are some whose act just cannot be revived
We sit and watch on helpless, as we know they won't survive

The audience sit patient now, discuss how this will end
Will the grand finale see them lose a parent, friend?
Will the different acts change how we lived our lives before?
Or will we make the same mistakes, be ignorant once more?

A change in act will always bring some grief and loss and fear
It's always hard to say goodbye to things that we hold dear
But change can make you walk down paths you've never seen before
To open up a whole new life behind your own front door

So now we must all sit tight and await the final act
Perhaps as we shout "Encore!" we could make a brand-new pact
To learn important lessons from this new show that we've seen
Grab the chance to learn, take charge, and wipe your old slates clean.

## *Fear*

I want to tell you something that I've put off up 'til now
I've worried how you'll take it; will you think me weak somehow?
It's something we don't talk about, it's something pushed away
We all try to ignore it - keep on coping every day

Yet Humans who admit to this find strength to carry on
Acknowledging they feel it helps them deal with what is wrong
In dealing with this big Taboo, emotions can be shared
To loved ones, friends, and colleagues - show support and that we care

This thing I feel is FEAR but I'm reluctant to admit
Each news report just scares me, and I cannot cope with it
But surely I can't be the only one who feels this way
So why put on a front? Why do we act like we're okay?

Surely this pandemic warrants' feeling helpless, sad
Surely we're allowed to say we're scared – it's nothing bad?
There's so much that we can't control, our lives have changed so much
So, sharing that we're scared sometimes provides us with a crutch

Support to hold us up when fear weighs heavy on our mind
Standing side by side to help each other and be kind
Sharing our bad moments, finding ways to help us through
So yes, I'm scared, but not alone - as now I've told you too.

## *Beauty is in the Eye of the Beholder*

The media would have us think the world is full of fear
That bad stuff's always happening, that danger's always near
They love to write a headline shouting "Terror" or "Disaster"
To make us read their stories, buy their papers even faster

Don't let your kids go out with friends, they might get shot or stabbed
Don't let them have their phone on view or else it might be grabbed
Don't let them go to nightclubs, they are terrifying places
Where drinks are spiked, and fights take place and acid's thrown in faces

Don't venture out alone as there is terror everywhere
Gang culture's taking over, and the Tories just don't care
Don't walk around the city as pollution's at its worst
And terrorists are everywhere, this country's really cursed

Now I am not an ostrich, I don't hide my head in sand
I do know these things happen and they make me feel so sad
But if we base our view of life on stories such as this
We'd never do a single thing, just think of all we'd miss

Think of all the joyful things that happen every day
The ones the news ignore because they're not full of dismay
Of laughter shared with friends, An act of kindness, that's a start
A baby being born, A partners' kiss that fills your heart

A tasty meal, A blissful sleep, A clear blue sky above
There's beauty all around us, nature's filled the world with love
Our favourite song, A lullaby, to see a loving smile
These things are happening all the time, they make our lives worthwhile

Terrorism, Shootings, Murder, War - we know they're there
But they're still in the minority, it's not that we don't care
But to focus on these bad events will stop us seeing clearly
That the world's still mostly beautiful - be sure to love it dearly.

# Part IV

# The Light at the End

# of the Tunnel

*Understanding Empathy*

*Connection and Kindness*

## *Stop, Look, Listen*

Hate is too big a pill to swallow
Hurt makes you ruminate and wallow
Stop
Talk and Listen

Learn to understand and question yourself
Ignorance is not bliss – just a curtain to hide behind
Stop
Listen and Learn

Listen to others, question them too
Hear what it is like to be them, not you
Stop
Show compassion, it's always in fashion

Learn to be kind to yourself
Kindness feels great, it carries no weight
Start
It's so much nicer than hate.

## The King of Words

There's one word in our language that I'd love you all to know
The impact of its' meaning should be taught to friend and foe
The difference it could make for humankind could change the game
Make people realise that when we're born, we start the same

To know what this word means will teach you what it is to feel
To pause and think before you speak your thoughts and make them real
To stop and dwell, reflect, before you roll out words of hate
Experience how they might taste from someone else's plate

To live your life in ways that prove you want to understand
Prepared to say, "I'm wrong", prepared to lend a helping hand
In educating others, asking questions when in doubt
Understanding different viewpoints makes your words land with more clout

This King of Words is **Empathy**, it's listening with intent
To put yourself in someone's shoes and understand what's meant
By absolutely hearing how it is to be that soul
To feel what walking in their shoes is like should be our goal

All babies are born innocent, they learn by what they see
So, if we teach them Empathy, imagine what could be
A world full of respect for how it feels to live as you
Where everyone's prepared to walk a mile in your own shoes

Some people's shoes are comfy, some they never seem to fit
Some shoes are not looked after, some will rub a little bit
Some people can walk miles, their feet just never seem to ache
But some take only tiny steps before their shoes will break

Let's start to walk together trying every shoe we meet
And see if we can find a way to all have happy feet
Let's get to understand why some shoes cause us so much pain
Learn Empathy - as Humans we are all one and the same.

## *The Commuter*

Twelve carriages of people, all commuters every day
We see the odd familiar face but mostly look away
We don't like making eye contact, we don't say "how are you"
We're British, we don't talk, we look intently at our shoes!

But have you ever wondered as you sit there on your phone
About those sitting next to you, of what goes on at home
Of whether they are happy, where they come from, what they do?
And whether their life's lovely, if they're better off than you?

Jo gets on at Thorpe Bay, perfect make-up on her face
Designer clothes, Designer Life, no hair is out of place
Her home looks like it comes straight from a glossy magazine
But Jo's just had a relapse after 2 years being clean

Mark gets on at Leigh and he is feeling really bad
Another row at home, he hit his wife, she got him mad
At least the kids were all upstairs, they won't have heard fists fly
At least that's what he tells himself whilst trying not to cry

Tim gets on at Benfleet, he is high up in IT
His colleagues all respect him, perfect wife, great family
But Tim he lost his dad last year, he isn't coping well
He tries to keep calm, carry on, but inside feels like hell

Mel's next on at West Ham, she is such a happy one
Always laughing, joking, such a smiley ball of fun
She's such a laugh and always loves a heavy drinking session
Red wine is such a great disguise to hide her own depression

So, look around the train today, I wonder who you'll see
Is Jo or Tim or Mel there, maybe Mark got on at Leigh?
Perhaps you're Tim who's struggling to deal with so much grief
Perhaps you're "happy" Mel who's hiding sadness underneath

The fact is we can't always know what someone's going through
Sometimes it's hard enough to live a day just being you
So next time that you travel try to keep an open mind
We've all got our own demons so it's best just to be kind.

## *Just Talk*

"Just Talk", we all hear, "It does helps you know"
"It's okay to not be okay"
But what should I say when my thoughts are so dark
That I can't see my way through today?

I'm told to reach out, tell you what it's about
That talking will help me to cope
But what do I do when I don't have the words
To explain that I've lost any hope

Where do I start when I can't feel my heart
When I'm numb and my mind just feels blank?
How can a chat get through any of that
To help fix all the things that have cracked?

"Just Talk" is a mountain that's too big to climb
My mouth seizes up, there's no sound
No words can describe what I'm feeling inside
I'm so ready to not be around

My answer to those who just can't find the words
Is to try "I need help" and that's all
It's one tiny step that I hope gives you time
To be caught by someone as you fall

Samaritans, work, your GP or a mate
It really does not matter who
"I need help" is the start of the path you must walk
Whilst you figure out how to heal you

Then after a while, you may reclaim your smile
Have new insight to spot those like you
Still stood in the dark with raw wounds in their heart
And you'll look in their eyes – say "Me too"

You can show them your scars, say "I've been where you are"
"It took time, but I've found a way through"
"I've sat with my pain, found my own voice again"
"Sit with me and I'll help find yours too."

# Part V

# The Other Side

*Learn to Feel*

*It will Help you to Heal*

## *Cry*

I watch the pain travel around your face
Looking for a place to settle
It pauses over your mouth
Dances over your lips, they quiver

A quick shiver as you drag in a breath
Preparing to swallow
Drinking down that thick emotion
Wash it down with some fake laughter

That incredibly painful gulp - like swallowing a fist
I can see how much it hurts to close the exit
"Sorry, no pain allowed out this way today!"
You bring the barriers down. And frown

Heavy breathing, with a chest that is heaving
A grimace like a Halloween mask
Fighting a silent battle to be strong
Why? It's so wrong!

Come sit with me, let those beautiful eyes fill
Welcome your pain in, acknowledge its' existence
Stop putting up resistance
Let tears do the job they were made for

Crying - the human medicine for sadness
The body's way to mend - it's our friend
So, when did we decide to keep it inside
Trapping our pain, ignoring it, neglecting it?

It hasn't made us strong! We are weaker!
Isolated in our grief - alone
Hiding behind grinning masks - alone
Desperate not to be caught out feeling!

My mind is left reeling at this world of pretend
If I'm sad then I want you to know it
If you're sad then I want you to show it
Tears cleanse, Crying mends
Emotion is the lotion of recovery.

## *Where there is Life*

When all around is chaos
When the only thing you see
Is hate and loss and helplessness
Keep holding on to me

When you want something to happen
But you don't know where to start
Have faith that I will help you
Hold me tight within your heart

When all the joy in life has gone
And all that's left is tears
Keep looking out for me each day
I'll help you face your fears

Always believe that I am here
To help you keep on going
Belief is what keeps me alive
And helps to keep you growing

My name is Hope and I am here
To give you strength to cope
This life of ours is beautiful
And where there's life, there's Hope.

## *Time for Change*

Change sometimes rearranges how I feel
Just for a while
Some days it tightens up my chest, can tighten up my smile
It spotlights insecurities - Anxiety takes hold
I start to doubt that I can cope with Change - old fears unfold

Change, it has a side that makes me wish that it would leave!
It bowls in uninvited, unannounced - Leaves me bereaved
It steals the life I love sometimes and floors this heart of mine
Its timing isn't something that I get to choose each time

Don't get me wrong, I do love Change, it feeds me, helps me grow
It guides me down new paths to places I would never know
When I decide to welcome Change, it mostly is my friend
But sometimes Change can leave me with a heart I need to mend.

Change never makes it easy when it makes you start again
It leaves you feeling vulnerable, susceptible to pain
Yet it cannot be avoided – life includes a Change or two
So, learn to accept Change and it will help you start anew.

## *Sit Tight*

Now is not forever
It's a moment in a day
And things you feel right now
Are just one part of what's Today

Today is just a moment
In a week of seven days
And a week is just a small part
Of a month that goes away

What happens in a month
Can change how things look in a year
The storm you thought would never pass
Will leave a sky that's clear

A worst day can feel permanent
Like sadness just won't leave
But get through now, today, a week
Allow yourself to breathe

Break up the pain
Divide it into now, today, this week
This month, this year - they 'll pass
'til "now" no longer feels so bleak

Sit tight, allow your feelings
To be heard and felt and then
Sit through today, a week, next month
'til you love life again.

## *That's Life*

Do you ever have those times in life when everything's just great?
When things are falling in to place and everyone's your mate
Your Partner is just perfect, and your child fills you with love
You've lost a tonne of weight – Your clothes, they fit you like a glove

Where work is going well, and you look forward to your day
And money is no object 'cos you've had a rise in pay
Your body is your temple and your belly's gone right down
You're feeling really happy, there's no reason for a frown

But do you get those times in life where nothing's going right
Where everything you touch turns into one big pile of shite?
You want to bin your Partner 'cos they're getting on your nerves
You want to bin your body 'cos it's full of lumps and curves!

Your child's a walking hormone who just eats and sleeps and moans
Whose life is watching Netflix, spending hours on their phone
Your job is crap, your boss a knob, you're desperate to just quit
The voice inside your head asks, "Why's my life such utter shit?"

The thing is life is just like that – it's ugly, gorgeous, bad
It's awesomeness, despairing, feeling like you're going mad
It's devastating, stunning, sadness, loss, and loss again
And then you get another day to do it all again

We moan and groan about life, but time comes round soon enough
When there's no more days to moan about a life that's been so tough
As long as you have laughed and lost and lived and loved and cried
You can shout as you bow out of life "Wow, what a fu*#ing ride!"

# Epilogue

## *I'm a Therapist But...*

I'm a therapist but...
I'm still just like you
I can still have those days that are hard to get through
I can still have old wounds that I find hard to heal
I can still have past hurts that I try not to feel

I still make bad choices that aren't for the best
I don't always take my life slowly and rest
I don't always do what is best for my mind
To family, loved ones, I'm not always kind

I can't change my past, it's what's made me this way
And sometimes the pain, it comes back for the day
It catches me out when I'm tired or I'm stressed
I re-act my old wounds and hope for the best

So how can I help if I still take steps back
And still have those times when I feel I might crack
Ironic to think I can help, you might say
When I don't walk the walk or feel great every day

The fact is there's no "cure" for loss or for pain
It comes and it goes, and it comes back again
Most days I love life and I really love me
So, I deal with the past when it hits painfully

Each time I work through it, I feel proud and free
I've shown I can swim through the stormiest sea!
I'm a therapist but... I am still just like you
Hold my hand and I'll help you to find your way through.

## *If I Knew....*

If I knew back then, what I know now
Would I still have pursued this big dream?
It's changed the way that I view my whole life
It's changed who I am, it would seem

I've wept for the wounds of my childhood
I've grieved for relationships ended
I've said my goodbyes to the ghosts of my past
And live with a heart mostly mended

Yet some days I miss that old version of me
As the "new me" can feel out of place
I try to relate to my family, friends
But we now walk a different pace

The way that I think has moved forward, evolved
My vision sees things others miss
I try to explain what I see, what I feel
Yet they stay back in ignorance - bliss!

I envy the fact that their world doesn't change
Whilst my old world has forever gone
I'll never go back to the ways I once knew
It feels great, but sometimes it feels wrong

A Therapists' role - what an honour it is
It's a choice I will never regret
But I do miss some parts of my funny old life
And my old self, I'll never forget.

## Therapy – The Real Thing

I can't tell you the difference therapy has made to my life – it's changed me forever.

It makes me sad that I didn't ask for help for so long and it makes me sad that so many of us STILL put on that brave face and pretend we're okay.

The importance of good mental health has come such a long way since I first experienced anxiety in the 90's, but we still have an awful long way to go in treating it with the same importance as our physical health.

Remember, there is nothing WRONG with you if you have poor mental health. It just means that you have experienced things in life that have had an effect on you as a human being.

In the same way that we are not immune from experiencing poor *physical* health, none of us are immune from experiencing poor *mental* health either.

So if you find yourself asking "What's WRONG with me?" try to re-phrase the question and instead, ask "What's HAPPENED to me? You might just see that life has thrown you some difficult punches and you need help getting back up again.

I'm going to finish with somebody else's words to sum up just what therapy can do for us – I'm using Nicole's words as, when I read her perspective, I just knew that I really couldn't have said it any better than this.

Proof that using someone else's words **CAN** help us – this is my hope with "The Little Book of Help".

*"For me, I don't think there was one magic ingredient that has suddenly made me feel loveable and functional. Rather it's been a series of processes that have helped in various ways.*

*So, I've learnt about how to relate better to others and express myself more clearly.*

I've learnt about the connection between my thoughts, feelings, and behaviours.

I've learnt an awful lot about self-care and being kind to myself.

I've learnt about why I developed patterns of behaviours that were self-sabotaging and how to develop better ones.

I've become much more able to sit with and process difficult and painful feelings rather than torture myself with negative thoughts and feelings. If I do have an emotional flashback, I know that it will pass and it's more related to the past than what's happening in the present.

I've learnt healthy ways to self-soothe, which for me include yoga and Pilates, EFT tapping, plenty of rest and relaxation.

I've learnt about limiting time I spend with people who are not good for me, and I am much more aware of the kind of people that I want in my life who are positive and life enhancing.

I've learnt that I can stand up for myself when I need to but that I can also walk away when it's more appropriate for me to do so.

I believe I'll always be a work in progress because I can't change the past. But I am at peace with that and can enjoy the journey more now!

For me therapy has been a process and each stage has provided a bit of the healing puzzle that has helped me to heal. But part of that healing is knowing that I don't have to be fixed for me to feel a whole lot better."

Nicole

# The End

# ABOUT THE AUTHOR

Samantha Lee is a BACP Registered Counsellor working in private practice. A large part of her experience covers the fields of domestic abuse and addiction.

She has a special interest in the effects of past trauma in Adult life, and a passion for Inner Child work, for which she has written online training courses for the UK Counselling Community.

Based near the coast in Essex, she's never happier than when she's out walking, taking photos with her trusty IPhone and spending time with her friends and family.

To find out more about her work, visit:

www.counselling4essex.co.uk

Printed in Great Britain
by Amazon